My Transition from Female to Male

by Thomas Nguyen

The Preview

This book was written to raise awareness of transgender people. It is a combination of my personal story and tips for dealing with the challenges of transitioning. I've written this book so that I can help parents and transgender individuals. I've done a lot of research before I began to write this book. I've gone through the transition process myself. I want to be a mentor for transgender teens and young adults.

The purpose of this book is to inform people about the challenges of being transgender, but also keep people interested in the content. I want to ensure that this book will be something that people will enjoy reading. At the back of this book, I have listed websites that people can refer to for additional information. I emphasize the importance of having access to more than one resource. I hope that you will find this book useful and informative.

Introduction

My name is Thomas Nguyen and I was born on November 20, 1992. I was born to my mother, Than Thi Nguyen, and father Than Huu Nguyen. I am the first child out of four children. I am a transgender female to male person living with a visual impairment. I wrote this book to educate the public, including other transgender people, about transitioning. The book is based on my experience and research about transitioning. I will begin by telling you about myself. I will explain how I began to transition and when I discovered by gender identity. I will also talk about living with a visual impairment while being transgender. I want this book to be informative, but also interesting. So I hope you enjoy this book.

I began to write this book because I wanted to tell people about being transgender. This is my experience and I do not represent all LGTBQ people. It took a lot of courage to come out to my family and my friends. It wasn't always easy. I took a lot of time to do research on what being transgender was. I searched for transgender resources on the internet and watched YouTube creators who were also transgender.

I knew from the time I was twelve years old that I wanted to be a boy. This began in the summer of 2005. Nobody in my family knew what being transgender was. Neither did myself. My Junior High School principal, Dean Michailides, told me about a friend who used to be David. Then, he transitioned to Angela.

My gender identity as a boy persisted throughout my teen years and early twenties. I was finally ready to come out at twenty-two years old. Transitioning wasn't going to be easy.

However, it was the right thing for me to do because it would help me become more comfortable in my own skin. I was born biologically female, but I was psychologically a boy from the time I was twelve years old. Prior to twelve, I was confused with my gender identity.

Besides being transgender, I'm also visually impaired. It affects how I interact with people and how I do everyday things. It also affects how I read. My gender identity and disability are the two rocks that I carry on my shoulder everyday. I carry the stones everyday because they are part of me. I think of the poem called "Pushing the Stone." It was the poem that a mother of an autistic son read on a youTube video named Barb. She left her job as an adjunct professor to care for him. To me, the stone is the burden of being transgender and disabled.

There are ups and downs to being visually impaired. The advantages are that I learn not to judge a book by its cover. I see the book for its content. I look at the outer cover as the outer beauty and the content as the inner beauty and personality. Also, I learned how to overcome my obstacle. This made me a stronger person. However, One of the disadvantages are not being able to get a driver's license. Also, finding employment is an issue. Today, people with disabilities face barriers in the work force. Employers are unaware about how to accommodate them. So, they are often overlooked.

I do not let being visually impaired define me. To me, it's just a disability that I have to learn to deal with on a daily basis. What I tell sighted people is that I function just as well as someone who is not visually impaired. I just do things differently.

One of my pet peeves is dealing with sighted people who just grab me out of nowhere when I am travelling somewhere in Edmonton. It annoys me and can scare me because I don't know who it is. Sighted people do this because they are trying to help. As a visually impaired person, I don't find it okay. I often have to teach sighted people how to guide me and what not to do when encountering someone like myself.

In 2012, I created a YouTube channel as a way to educate the sighted world about visual impairment. I also wanted to help other visually impaired people deal with their disability and encouraged them to be as independent as possible.

After I came out as transgender to my friends and family, I started to come out on YouTube. I began to make videos explaining the challenges of coming out. I also would mention about starting on hormones and going through the name change.

Being transgender means that I was assigned female at birth, but identify as male. It isn't easy being transgender. I still get misgendered at times. When I am in public, I often have to correct people when they misgender me. I don't see being transgender as a disorder. Instead, I look at it as being part of who I am.

The Foster Home

I remember as early as five years old when I had to live in a foster home. It was like being taken away from my parents. I remember a lady going to my parents' house and and took me into her car. I had no idea where I was even going. The next thing I knew was I was at another house. It was strange to me. I remember missing my mom a lot and wanted to go back.

On the weekends, my foster mom drove me to stay with my biological mom. The best thing was playing with my sisters. I remember playing Wee 3 and school with them. On Sundays, I would have to go back to my foster home.

I stayed in the foster home for five years when I lived in Vancouver. In 2003, when I was 10 years old, I went back to living with my biological family. I wanted to go back with them because I didn't want to live at a foster home anymore. I wanted to be with my biological family. The benefit of being with my biological parents was that I learned how to speak Vietnamese fluently again. Also, I got to bond with my sisters.

My foster mom was named veronica. She was a good parent. She put me in my place whenever I misbehaved. I didn't like it as a child. Now, as an adult, I appreciate her for disciplining me and putting me in my place as a child. Otherwise, I would turn out to be entitled. She was also very caring. She bought me lots of toys to play with. She also packed my lunch for school every week day.

I was a stubborn child. I remember when my foster mom had to force me to take my medicine. It tasted disgusting. I hated my medicine. When I was nine years old, I became willing to cooperate with her. I was also more cooperative with the dentist. Before, i hated it when the dentist had to put stuff in my mouth.

I had to address my foster mom as "Mom" and not her name. She said that it was impolite to do so. To this day, I still call her "Mom". It's like having two moms. I have her and my biological mother.

Her husband was named Albert. I called him dad because it was considered respect. He looks at me as his own child. I'm very fortunate that my foster parents were loving and caring.

My foster mom put me in Girl Guides when I was eight years old. I was a brownie. When I was nine years old, I became a guide. I stopped attending girl guides when I was ten years old. One thing that girl guides taught me was to learn how to make friends. My favourite part was selling cookies, singing songs, and doing crafts. I also liked that I could earn badges.

After I left my foster home, I still kept in touch with my foster mom. To this day, I still contact her, but not as often. Now, her foster home is now a group home for adults with disabilities.

Early Childhood

As a child, I was very playful and full of energy. I also played with any toy. I did not know the difference between a boy toy and a girl toy. I remember as young as five years old, I was confused with my gender identity. My foster brother, Neil, had severe autism. I remember touching his genitals when he laid on the floor. I wondered why his genitals stuck out. When I was in my room at my foster home, I began to explore my genitals. I wondered to myself, Why was mine different than his?"

I remember when my biological mom put me in a dress. I did not understand why I had one on. I think I was six years old at that time. Also, I remember as early as Grade 1, I would get confused between boys and girls. I did not understand what the difference was. In Grade 4, I tried to be girly. Back then, I thought being girly meant being a perfect princess. I grew out of that phase when I was in Grade 5.

I have attended four elementary schools during my childhood. I attended two in Vancouver, one in Calgary, and one in Edmonton. I grew up with my biological family moving from house to house, even during my stay at my foster home. I was too young to know why this was happening. As I got older, I would hear stories from one of my sisters about my biological family's house constantly getting robbed. That was why they had to move.

In Grade 5 and 6, my favourite thing to do during recess was playing on the gliders and monkey bars. I would play on them so much that I would end up with blisters. When I was on the monkey bars, I would pretend to be a monkey and make monkey noises.

I stayed in Vancouver from the time I was 1 to 10 years old. My parents had my sisters in Vancouver. Their names are An, Christine, and Kathleen. I was the only one out of four children that was born in Edmonton.

My family and I moved to Calgary in 2003. My sisters and I attended Annie Foote school. This was the first time ever going to the same school as my sisters. We lived in Calgary for a year. In 2004, we moved to Edmonton and all four of us attended Princeton Elementary school. I attended there during my Grade 6 year. In Junior High, I attended Balwin School. In high school, I attended and graduated from Eastglen Composite High School.

As a teenager, I had to grow up faster than most people my age. Teachers expected us to be mature in junior high, so I tried to act like a grown up. I had responsibilities parents were supposed to have, such as making sure my two younger sisters were up and ready for school. My dad expected me to do this every school day. After all, I was the oldest.

I developed depression in the middle of Grade 7. Often, I felt like committing suicide. I have experienced emotional and psychological abuse from my dad and my educational assistant, Donna Konschuh. My teachers did not take into account that I had depression. Neither did I. I was just a kid and thought that it was just stress. I was powerless because I did not have the guts to stand up to an adult. At the same time, I was sheltered by Donna Konschuh and I found it really annoying. When she snapped at me, she used the PMS excuse. All of this over sheltering did not do me any favours because it made me scared of the real world and I was not into taking risks. However, when I entered high school, I had to learn to take risks to help myself grow. I had a different educational assistant named Angela Roppo. What I learned from her was that it was really important to learn to overcome struggles and hardships in order to be prepared for the real world. Also, I had to learn to be a teenager and be less serious.

I fought for my independence as a teenager because I wanted to be like other teenagers. My mom was overprotective and worried about me because of my visual impairment. I wanted to prove to her that I could be as independent as a person who is sighted. I often took the public transit without her knowing because I was tired of her overprotectiveness. I lied about taking DATS so she wouldn't worry. DATS stands for Disabled Adult Transit Service.

I had my first job when I was 17 years old. I taught piano for over seven years. When I first taught, my piano school was at Londonderry Mall. In 2013, we had to move to Northgate Mall. I was an ear training and scales teacher. I liked having a job because it gave me some independence and it empowered me to be able to go out in the community and be productive. It made me feel like a normal teenager working a part-time job. This meant that I didn't have to ask my parents for money. Also, it gave me something to do.

Growing up with a visual impairment, I had to learn to do things differently than sighted people. I had to learn to feel for things, read braille, and navigate using a white cane. I also had to learn how to do things safely without the benefit of sight. Usually, I was the only visually impaired person at school.

Adolescent Years

My adolescent years were tough. Besides having to grow up so fast, I went into a deep depression. The truth was my teachers did not have any knowledge about depression. Often, I left class a lot when I had depression. The truth was I also didn't know what this was. I thought to myself: "Oh, maybe I'm just having a bad day." Mrs. Konschuh often used the PMS excuse. To me, this did not make any sense. Whenever she bitched at me, she would use the period excuse. I cannot stand women who blame everything on their period. My biggest pet peeve was that Mrs. Konschuh did not take it seriously when I said that I wanted to commit suicide. She just dismissed this as "so called adolescent thoughts." To this day, I never speak to her or contact her.

I felt like I was forced into being an adult before I was ready. On some levels, I was mature and responsible. However, at the same time, I was just a kid. I was still learning how to deal with my emotions. When I was in high school, Ms. Roppo told me, "You need to learn how to be a teenager." I was too serious in general. I also did not get jokes and humour. I took things literally. I never understood why I was the way I was. Ms. Roppo suspected that I could be on the autism spectrum. It was hard to believe I could have autism. After all, I functioned just like everyone else and I did not have many of the signs of autism.

When I was in Grade 9, I started my own diary journals. I found that journaling my thoughts on paper was a way to vent out my anger.

Apparently, most of the entries were forgotten at my high school. I did not go back to journaling my thoughts until I started university. Most of my entries from 2013 or later were about how my first year of university was going.

The worse thing that happened during my teen years was going through the puberty of the wrong gender. I knew from the time I was twelve years old that I wanted to be a boy. I was born in the wrong body. My dad was totally against me trying to change to being a boy. He told me that I was 100% girl.

When I told my teachers that I wanted to be a boy, they told me that girls were better and boys were trouble makers. The teachers who said that were hypocritical feminist women who were anti-male. I despise people like that. They often thought that I was a tomboy and that I would grow out of it.

I did not grow out of it. In high school, I tried things like wearing purses and dealing with long hair. I knew something wasn't right. I did not know what transgender was back than. Mr. Michailides, my junior high principal, told me about a friend who transitioned from male to female. I told him that I wanted to transition to. However, I did not have the support or resources to be able to transition early. Plus, I was still a teenager. I did not have the mental capacity to think about the risks of transitioning.

In high school, I tried to be something that I wasn't. I tried to act more like a woman because people told me that I was a woman. I did not have the courage to come out to people and tell them that I was a boy trapped in a girl's body. Worse of all, I felt forced into being like one. I was expected to leave my hair long and wear girl clothes. During my high school graduation, I had to wear a dress. It was no fun because I could not sit with my legs apart. Plus, I found high heels lame and uncomfortable.

During my late teens, I read a story on Readers Digest about a man who came out to his wife as transgender. Before he came out, he would cross-dress in secret and wear his mother's clothes. When his wife found his makeup, she thought that he had an affair with another woman. This was when he told her that he was the other woman. He transitioned from he to she and from Rodger to Paige. The unfortunate news was that her wife divorced from her ant it cost them their marriage.

I felt sad for Paige. However, reading her story has encouraged me to do some research about being transgender. The more I spent time on the internet researching, the more I realized that this was me. I was transgender. I was unsure about how I was going to come out and how to tell my family. I continued to do research until I understood what transgender was.

Learning about being transgender has taught me that sex and gender were not the same. For nineteen years of my life, I grew up thinking that they were the same. However, it turns out that sex is our biology and gender is what is in our brain.

When I was researching about being transgender, I also learned that in order for me to transition, I would need to take testosterone. This meant that it would allow me to develop secondary male characteristics. I also had to consider my decision to have surgery. I wanted to do it before pursuing a relationship because I did not want to end up in the same situation that Paige was in. She had a wife and children. I could imagine how hard it was for them to adapt, especially the wife.

How I Picked the name Thomas

I originally got the name Thomas from Thomas and Friends, a train show for little kids. I became obsessed with that name. I wanted to be called "Thomas." My teachers would not call me that because it was a boy's name and it was not my legal name. They thought that it was just a nickname.

When I began to transition, I did not come out to my family until I was twenty-two years old. It took my family time to get used to my new name. My dad was against calling me "Thomas". He was also against the idea of me transitioning. He would resist calling me by my new name and still called me by my birth name. I became angry and hostel at my dad.

It took my EA's and professors a while to get used to my new name. The challenges was that I still needed to write my birth name as my signature and I hated it. I found that my birth name did not reflect who I was as a man. When my name was legally changed to Thomas, things were easier. I could write my new name as my signature and everyone I met would know me as Thomas.

One of the challenges was learning how to be patient with my family, especially my mom. She's know me as my old name for over twenty years and it was hard for her to adjust. I often got frustrated when she referred to me by my birth name. I would correct her every single time. At least my mom was trying to adapt while my dad resisted.

I chose the name, Thomas, because I could imagine identifying myself as that name. It was the name that reflected my gender identity. I do not regret this decision. It was worth the trouble to go through the legal name change process so I could live as Thomas full time. This meant that the government officials would recognize me as Thomas.

The challenges of going through the name change process was filling out the application, getting my fingerprints done, and waiting for the results to come in the mail. The worse thing was waiting for the name change process to finish after submitting the finger print results with the application. It costed almost $200 for both the name change and fingerprints.

After the name change was complete, I felt that a ton was lifted off my shoulder. This meant less confusion and everyone would know me by my new name.

To me, having a male name was a passage to passing as a man. My name was more aligned with my gender identity. To me, the name, Thomas, is very masculine and strong. To this day, my mom calls me by my new name and she tries her best to buy me men's clothes. I am very proud of her for trying.

I did not like women's clothes because they often showed my feminine figure. They did not reflect who I was. I got rid of them while I began to transition because I wanted to pass as a man. I wanted my clothes to reflect who I was. The challenges of looking for men's clothes was that they were often too big. They did not fit me. I went to many stores until I could find one that sold smaller clothes for men. I realized that being a small man was a disadvantage because I couldn't wear the clothes that the big men wore.

Living as a woman, clothes were an advantage because I could fit smaller clothes. Most women's clothing were designed for small women. The most annoying thing was I would hear women say how lucky I was to be small built. The truth was I didn't want to be that way. It took me years to learn to accept that this was the way I was.

As a transgender man, I find that having periods contribute to my gender disforia. A lot of times, I think to myself, "Men are not supposed to have periods." When I have a period, I feel devastated and depressed.

I bind my chests using a binder or a sports bra. I am still thinking about surgery. I understand it's risky and I need to make sure that this is what I want to do. Binding my chest is a lot less risky and I think i'm just going to put off surgery until I'm financially stable. I'm thinking that I want to get top surgery and have the key hole surgery done on my chest. I heard that it has less scarring. However, it's not the most suitable for transgender men with larger chests.

Bottom surgery is still ways away. It would be nice to have a functional penis created. However, I'm worried about the risks.

My Medical Transition

I wanted to start taking testosterone because I wanted to start developing secondary male characteristics. I wanted to be like other men. This meant that taking hormones would allow me to get a deeper voice, grow facial hair, and have my body fat redistributed into more of a male pattern. Before I made my decision to start hormones, I did as much research as I could so that I would know what to expect. I wanted to prepare myself as much as I could.

During my research, I learned that if I was to go on testosterone, my sex drive would increase and my body fat would redistribute into a more male pattern. I also learned that my clitterus would grow, but it won't be the same as a full penis.

During my research, I learned that injecting testosterone would be more effective than patches or testosterone jell because testosterone would last longer in the body. I got a lot of this information from femaletomale.org. I found that website very helpful because it provided me with the information that I needed in order to transition medically. Unfortunately, that website does not exist anymore. Also, I learned about how testosterone could affect your singing voice. To be honest, after a few months on testosterone, I started to loose the ability to sing the higher notes in the fifth octave. My voice started to crack as if I was going through puberty. Testosterone gave me an advantage because I could now sing the lower notes. It took a while to get used to my new singing range.

Before I started on testosterone, I had to get Dr. Wong to refer me to an endocrinologist. I was so glad that he was willing to to this for me. It took about a year for me to get referred to the endocrinologist. In February of 2017, I had my first appointment with him. The endocrinologist was Dr. Romney. I had to get my blood work done before I could start on hormones.

When I first began hormones, I was put on 75 mG every three weeks. I had to be put on a low dose because my body needed the time to get used to the external testosterone ;being injected. Primarily, my body has been mainly producing estrogen.

I started to notice a change in my voice after four months on testosterone. As of August 2017, I was already six months on testosterone. I have not started growing facial hair. What I also noticed while being on testosterone was that my body odour smelled so bad. I sweat more than I was before beginning testosterone. I have to apply deodorant more than once. Sometimes, up to three times in a day.

To be honest, I find that women's deodorant is terrible because it does not last as long as men's. However, the exceptions the Secret brand for women. I did not like the fact that the women's deodorant smelled so fruity. When I put it on, I would smell like fruit. No thanks!

Being on testosterone, I find that my voice cracks while I try to sing the higher notes in the fifth octave. I find it easier to reach the lower notes. I noticed that testosterone started to have an effect on the singing voice after I tried to sing after four months of bing on hormones. It's a challenge, but an interesting experience. I feel like a teenager again. I felt like this was my second chance to go through puberty again. However this time, I would be going through male puberty.

I prey that my periods will stop. I hate getting periods as a man because I find that it causes gender disforia. No man ever wants to go through the wrong puberty. Also, no man wants to have to carry some hygiene supplies just because of the period. According to my research, I heard that my period would stop after being on testosterone. However, the time it takes for the period to stop varies from individual to individual. It depends on different transgender men and how their bodies respond to the testosterone.

I'm going to get used to shaving my face once I start to notice facial hair. Oh well, that's part of being a man. I will ask my male friends to show me how to shave my beard before I start growing one. I'll also have to get used to having hair all over my body, including my chests, stomach, and back.

My experience overall has been positive. I started getting some secondary male characteristics. I now experience a more narrow range of emotions. I'm either happy, frustrated, or angry. I don't tear up as much as I used to. On the other hand, I tend to get angry very easily. I'm often very horny. I also tend to feel aggression. The negative side of being on testosterone is that it puts me at risk for heart disease, high blood pressure, high cholesterol, and heart attack. This puts me in the risk profile of a man. I also notice that I gained some pounds while being on testosterone. Once in a while, I get my weight checked at my doctor's office. I do my best to eat right so I can maintain a healthy weight. Honestly, I don't always eat healthy. However, I want to make sure I get enough vitamins.

Singing during T

Before I began testosterone, I used to be able to sing an octave higher. In my early twenties, I became interested in learning some vocal techniques. I've learned some of them on YouTube. In MacEwan Residence, I used to sing a long to a lot of my songs on my playlist. I have some videos of myself singing before I began hormone therapy. I would say I was around a high alto. I would spend about two hours a day singing in my dorm. It did help me improve my singing.

Before I began testosterone, I was worried about how it would affect my voice. I was worried about the potential to never be able to sing again. Despite my fears, I knew that the decision to take testosterone was right for me. After I began testosterone, I noticed some changes after a few weeks. It felt as if something was scratching in my throat. My vocal cords were starting to thicken. It was strange to see that my voice was changing. This meant I had to get used to my new singing voice. My voice began to crack as if I was going through puberty. My range was beginning to change. Also, the tone of my voice was starting to change. I was starting to sound like a tenor.

Since I was becoming a tenor, I had to find songs that were suitable for tenors to sing. Britney Spears songs were not suitable for me anymore. I also found that Minh Tuyet songs were becoming too high for me. I had to be patient with myself because I needed time to explore my voice all over again. I had to find out where I was comfortable and where I was not comfortable. My bridging location was changing. The advantage of starting T, however, was that I was able to reach some of the lower notes.

I wanted to take things slowly, especially when it came to my voice. I didn't want to risk my voice quality. I still wanted to be able to sing. I sometimes wish that I was a baritone. I love that baritones can sing some of the lower notes. However, I'm willing to accept my tenor voice. I choose to look at the positive side of being a tenor. Since most male pop singers are tenors, I have an advantage. If I were a baritone, it would be more difficult for me to reach the notes that the tenors reach with ease.

I love to karaoke. I especially love doing it with my sisters and other family members. Sometimes, I karaoke in bars. I love to sing BackStreet Boys songs a lot. I also like to sing Hadaway and Justin Timberlake.

Being on testosterone has helped me relate to teen boys who are going through puberty. Now, I know what's like for my voice to deepen. The experience wasn't as bad as I thought it would be. My overall experience of being on testosterone was more positive than negative. I'm fortunate that I'm still able to sing. What's interesting is that I get to look at my YouTube Videos of myself before T and after T. My voice has changed a lot. It has dropped at least an octave. If I never began T, I wouldn't be a tenor now. I'd still sound like myself before T.

Being a tenor is great because there are lots of songs for tenors to sing. When you are a tenor, the high notes are no problem for you. After all, tenors shine in the higher notes. Pop songs, for example, are great for tenors. Tenors are found in quires. I think that every voice type should be celebrated. I'd like to keep my tenor voice for as long as I can. I'm happy with it and that's all it matters.

My voice is an instrument that I carry with me all the time. It's inside me. I can practice with my voice anywhere I wish. With a piano, however, I can't take it anywhere. It's way too big and way too heavy. A recorder is more portable. However, I find that the voice is a more unique musical instrument than any other musical instrument. Every voice has its own vocal signature.

What I notice that a lot of transgender guys' voices tend to be tenor voices. I've listened to other transgender males on their YouTube channels. My guess is that our larynx tends to be a bit smaller and we have thinner vocal cords. This is just an educated guess. I've never heard voices of transgender guys who were baritones or basses. So, I can't say for sure if there are any of us that sing bass who are female to male.

Overall, being female to male seems easier than being male to female. At least with myself, testosterone deepens the voice. In contrast, taking estrogen will not make a transgender woman's voice higher. What transgender woman wants to sound like a bass or baritone?

Do I Want to have Children?

Well, I've been thinking about this question frequently. I want to, but I am not interested in carrying the pregnancy, even though I could. If I have a girlfriend or wife someday, I am planning to have her carry the child. However, a sperm donor will be necessary because the depressing fact is I can't make sperm. However, I just have to accept the fact.

I learned about labor and delivery in Biology 30 and I heard it hurts. I never want to experience it. I have no interest what so ever. I also learned about pregnancy. I can't imagine myself being able to handle it. I just don't have the emotions to deal with it.

I don't think storing my eggs would be the most effective because first of all, it is expensive. If I were to freeze my eggs, their quality would degrade over time. That is why I would rather have my wife or girlfriend use her eggs.

I think when my children are old enough, they will be able to understand that they were conceived using donor sperm. However the question is: What is the best way to tell them? I think at three or four years old, they would be too young to understand. I'm planning to tell them when they are old enough to understand the biology of baby making.

To be honest, I can't imagine trying to get pregnant like Thomas Beatie did. He was also a transgender man. I just don't want to go through any legal issues like he did. I don't want to make things even more confusing. I'm afraid that people would make negative comments about a man being pregnant. People would question me and ask me how a man could get pregnant. After all, men are not supposed to get pregnant. Only women are supposed to get pregnant.

From my biology knowledge, a cisgender man cannot get pregnant because he does not have the reproductive anatomy to do so. A transgender woman also can't get pregnant because she would have the same reproductive anatomy as a cisgender man. She could father children if she still has her male reproductive organs. On the other hand, cisgender women and transgender men can get pregnant if they still have their female reproductive organs. That's biology.

I'm thinking about getting a hysterectomy in the future. However, it's a big decision because once I get the procedure done, I will not be able to have biological children. I will have to be on hormones for the rest of my life. On the good side, I would never have to worry about periods and pregnancy.

Another option I'm considering is adoption. There are so many children who are born to parents who can't take care of them emotionally and financially. Kids are often put in one foster home after another. The system is pretty messed up. Regardless of which option I choose, I'll still love them as my own kids.

First of all, I don't want to have kids if I can't financially support them. Kids are so expensive. You're financially obligated to support them until they reach 18 years of age. Parents are still supporting kids well into their twenties today. I don't want to have a kid and financially struggle to raise him or her. I don't think it's fair to the kid. I would rather raise my kid in a stable environment, not in a broken home. I don't want to be a single dad. I rather raise a kid with a wife, not a common law or cohabiting partner. If I still decide that I would not have kids, I'm okay with it. Besides, there's no guarantee that my kids will take care of me during old age. Plus, kids eat up your finances.

What washroom do you use?

This is one of the questions that I get asked by people after I mention to them that I am transgender. To be honest, I find this to be a personal question because I prefer not to answer such questions like this one. I feel awkward when people ask me which bathroom I use.

Some transgender people use the gender neutral washrooms while others use the men's or women's washroom. I honestly think that we have the right as humans to use the washroom of the gender they identify as. When I first started using the men's washroom, I got mistaken as a woman. Passing was challenging enough because I did not have the secondary male characteristics yet and my voice was not masculine enough. I had a neutral voice. I hated the women's washroom because women often socialize in there and they often do their makeup. Men on the other hand just go in to do their business and leave when they are done.

I have used urinals before, but I choose not to use them, especially public ones. I always fear for my safety because there are transphobic people everywhere, especially ones from older generations.

I heard of people in the US trying to pass bills that would prevent transgender people from using their preferred bathroom. I think that it is an act of discrimination because you are telling them to use the bathroom of their biological sex. Sex and gender are not the same thing and I do not think that anyone should have the right to tell other people which bathroom to use. Jazz Jennings, a transgender girl, was banned from using the girls bathroom at school because she was assigned male at birth. She had to use the nurse's bathroom. She hated using the nurses bathroom because kids often puked in there.

I am glad that there are gender neutral washrooms because they make it safer for gender nonconforming people like myself to go to the washroom. However, I don't get why there needs to be a single washroom for men and for women. Single washrooms should be gender neutral and public washrooms can be kept gender segregated. In a public washroom, women and men might feel awkward sharing the same washroom. So it makes sense for public washrooms to be separate for men and women.

When did you decide to be transgender?

To be honest, I did not choose to be transgender. It was something that I discovered when I was twelve years old. I knew that I wanted to be a boy. Back then, I didn't know what transgender was. At thirteen years of age, I learned from my Junior High principal about a friend who transitioned from male to female. I thought to myself: "I want to get the surgery so that I could be a boy." I was not mature enough to realize the consequences of the surgery.

My dad was totally against me wanting to be a boy. He told me that I was 100% girl. All of my teachers did not understand why I wanted to be a boy, neither did my dad.

I tried to fit into the gender that I was raised to be. I tried purses because I thought that they would make me more womanly. By nineteen years of age, I new 100% that I was transgender. Researching on the internet and reading websites about transgender people gave me the power to come out to my family, friends, and professors. I didn't come out fully until I was twenty-two years old. When I first told my mom, "I'm a boy", she was shocked and didn't say anything. She had no idea what transgender was.

I legally changed my name to Thomas so that my name would reflect my gender identity. I do not have a middle name anymore. I used to, but I decided to drop it because the middle name I was given at birth was for Vietnamese girls. I knew I wasn't a cisgender woman; I was a transgender man.

My parents had a hard time with my name change at first because they've known me by my birth name for over two decades. They gave me that name. It was hard to be patient, especially with family because I expected them to get used to the new name quickly. My dad, like typical Asian dads, was very stubborn and was stuck in his ways of thinking. He grew up with a certain way of what gender was. His thinking was, "You're either born a boy or a girl. There is no such thing is transgender." It took him about two years to accept that his was who I really was, a man trapped in a woman's body.

Unfortunately, there are people who do not think that transgender exists. They don't want to learn about what transgender is because they are closed minded. They're too ignorant and want to believe what they want to believe. However, the good news is that awareness of transgender people is slowly spreading. People are starting to become accepting. Of course, we don't live in a perfect world. We're always going to deal with issues and challenges. It helps us grow as persons.

Starting on testosterone has started to help me be one day closer to passing as a man everyday. I noticed a change in my voice after being on the hormone for six months. However, the cons of being on testosterone is that my body odour smells really bad and I get more acne on my face. I can't wait to grow facial hair, but I'm not looking forward to shaving.

Changing my gender on my ID was more challenging than changing my legal name because I had to find a doctor that would be willing to write a letter confirming my request for the gender change. It took me three tries to change my gender legally because my doctor missed some information on my letter. After the third try, my gender was finally changed. I felt more confident because whenever I show my ID, I would not have to have people mistake me as a woman.

After you came out, was your family supportive?

My sisters were the most supportive people in my family. So were my friends. With support, I felt empowered to make the decision to legally and medically transition. I would not be where I am now without support.

At the time of my dad not supporting me during my transition, I often would boy caught him. I felt that if he did love me, he should have been supportive no matter what. I would often swear in French whenever I was mad at him, but it didn't make things better at all. All that swearing has made me even more bitter towards him. It was also hard for me to get over the fact that he has abused me emotionally and psychologically for over a decade. He would often label me as being stupid and he would say that I was a bad person multiple times, especially in my teen years.

At the age of twenty-one, I decided to move out of my parents' home because I felt like I had to get away from the abuse from my dad. I lived in MacEwan Residence for two years. Living there has given me the training wheels to live on my own. It gave me the sense of independence. The essential things that I learned how to do was making sure I had groceries, pay rent, and sharing the apartment with a room mate. I also learned to get in the habit of making sure to keep the common area clean.

The down side of living in MacEwan Residence was that I had to put up with party kids who would just have their music up loud until late at night. I found it very distracting, especially when I was trying to study. During my second year at MacEwan Residence, I lived in a bachelor's suite. I had to deal with the guys next door who frequently had their music up loud until midnight. I often had to phone the front desk to complain.

I began to come out to people at MacEwan Residence as Transgender, even to my house coordinators. They respected my wish to be referred to by my male name, even though it was not official yet.

So far, I did not come across professors and classmates who were transphobic. I'm very fortunate to know that they are very supportive and know about my transgender identity. If I ever come across a transphobic person, I just won't associate with them. I want to hang out with people who are inclusive to transgender and other gender nonconforming people. MacEwan University has did the right thing by allowing gender nonconforming people to have their preferred names on their ID cards and have the option to identify as male, female, or other gender. I feel like the university has did a good job to change to being more trans inclusive. I sure hope that other universities will do the same thing. I feel like universities and colleges should be more inclusive to gender minorities because the environment will be more welcoming for those who do not identify in the binary gender category.

What I would like to see is more gender neutral bathrooms in public places, such as restaurants. That way, it makes it safe for people like myself in order to use the bathroom without people questioning our gender. I heard of cases on transgender people getting beaten up in public washrooms. I can't even imagine being beaten up in a men's bathroom by someone who suspects that I'm transgender. I also can't imagine how hard it would be for a transgender woman to use the women's bathroom without getting stared at. I sure hope that the bathroom bill in the US will not be passed. I'm glad that there is no bathroom bill in Canada.

I can't imagine government officials standing outside of public bathrooms checking our birth certificates and asking us for a physical examination of our bodies. That would be an invasion of privacy. Also, it would be humiliating, especially for gender minorities. It would not be safe for anyone to use the public bathrooms. I just don't understand why there needs to be a bathroom bill. It will just make things worse. I would feel threatened as a transgender person if there was a bathroom bill.

I do not like Trump because he is a scammer and only cares about himself. He made a commercial about Trump University, which turned out to not be a real university at all. He is racist and he also is transphobic. He even banned transgender people from joining the military. I think that this is an act of discrimination against trans people because he is infringing on their rights to choose to join the military..

There are things that you should never say to transgender people. Never ask "Do you still have a penis?" or "What's between your legs?" These are inappropriate questions. Never ask a transgender person what heir birth name is because they may not be comfortable about telling you. Also, do not ask if you can see their pre-transition photos. Do not ask about how a transgender person has sex. Sex is a private thing and it would put them in an awkward situation.

Imagine being asked how you have sex. How would it make you feel? You may feel awkward. You may feel that the information is personal. Also, what if people asked you about your private area? Would you want to be asked what washroom you use? Of course not!

What I do when people refer to me by the Wrong Gender

I try to politely correct people when they refer to me by the wrong pronouns I prefer people to refer to me with male pronouns. Sometimes, I get impatient when people mess up.

However, it is not my intention to. I feel like transgender people have to work harder in order to pass as a man or woman, especially when they recently began transitioning. In my case, I had to get of all my girl clothes, cut my hair short, change my name and my gender on my legal documents. I need to take testosterone in order to develop like a man because my body can't do this naturally. I would like to have a deeper voice so that people do not mistake me as a woman. I want to be more passable as a man.

My mom has a hard time understanding why I need testosterone. She feels that natural is better and that I should just leave my body the way it is. I hope that some day, she will realize why I began testosterone. This decision was made by me 100% and I am tired of her making assumptions that people told me to take testosterone. I have my own mind and I can make responsible decisions for myself. I don't need anyone to decide for me what I should do with my life. I need to do what is best for me and what makes me happy. However, at the same time, I have to make sure to keep myself safe and to not associate with transphobic and homophobic people.

I had a transphobic bus driver once. As I was talking on my phone with my mom, he interrupted me and told me to hang up. He did not care that he referred to me by female pronouns. I complained to the city of Edmonton about him and told them what happened. To this day, I never had to encounter him again.

If I had a transphobic professor, I would not want to continue taking his class because I would not want to be humiliated in front of the whole class. I would tell the dean about their negative attitudes towards gender nonconforming people. I would quit their class regardless of what class it is.

What I want people to know about Transgender People

Every transgender person goes through transition at their own pace. No two of us are alike. Some people choose to go through surgery while others choose not to. Some people choose hormones to transition.

Gender reassignment surgery comes in different parts and may take years to complete. It is irreversible and may make us sterile for the rest of our life. Everyone is ready at different times to have the surgery.

Transgender people who's family and friends are not accepting are more at risk of committing suicide. Those of you who have a transgender family member or know of someone who is transgender should open your minds about gender nonconformity. I'm not asking at all for you to change your minds; I'm only asking you to open them. I think people from older generations would have a hard time with this concept because they grew up in a norm where gender nonconformity was frowned upon. I think most of us have grown up with the concept of binary gender. We learn how to associate our biological sex with our gender.

I can tell you that I grew up thinking that sex and gender were the same. I remember that people would say that you were born either a boy or a girl and no in between. I never heard about what transgender was until I was in my teen years. I often would hear people say that pink was for girls and blue was for boys.

I played with almost any toy because I didn't know the difference between a boy toy and a girl toy. I played with trucks, trains, dolls, blocks, etc. No one had told me, "You can't play with this because it's a boy toy." I liked to build with blocks and I often pretended to fix things. I would play with water guns.

If I often would sit with my legs apart because I hated sitting with my legs crossed like a lady. I did not like it when my mom told me that I was supposed to sit with my legs together because that was how women were supposed to sit. I often rebelled because I refused to sit like that. I wanted to sit the way boys sat. My teachers and parents assumed that I would grow out of acting like a boy and that it was just a phase.

If I got to transition early, I'm convinced that I would be able to grow a few more inches. I would be put on hormone blockers to suppress my natural female puberty. However, because of a lack of understanding from my parents and teachers in the past, I had to wait to transition at a time that was safe for me. Researching about being transgender has helped me gain enough knowledge. This allowed me to tell people why I wanted to transition and why it would do me good. Transitioning has helped me be a more confident person. It also helped me to become more outgoing. This empowered me to do what made me feel like my true self.

Some transgender people cannot transition at all due to their family, friends, and other people not accepting them. It's okay to agree or disagree with their choice to transition. One thing that is not okay to do is to tell them that they are not allowed to transition or that God made them a boy or girl. It's their body and once they reach the age of majority, it is legally their choice.

It is up to transgender people to decide when they are ready to transition. It's good to encourage them, but avoid pressuring them. All you can do is be as supportive as possible. Do not tell people that they are transgender, unless they are okay with it. Also, do not pressure them into surgery if they are not ready. When they are ready, they will come out to you. Help them find resources to help them learn about their transgender identity. If you are transphobic, I suggest you keep your opinions to yourself because those opinions are often hurtful to transgender people. Honestly, I try not to associate with transphobic people. I do not let them tell me that I'm a freak. I do not like it when they say, "God made you a woman or man and this was what he wanted you to be."Our gender does not always have to match our biological sex. I think that it's important for people to realize that in increase their transgender awareness.

What if you told me that you were gay or lesbian? Just pretend for a second that I was a family member that has known you for years. Imagine how I might react. If I was supportive and open-minded, I would be accepting of your sexual orientation. I would not think about you as being weird. I also would not think that being gay was a bad choice you made. Being gay was just something you discovered and didn't choose. If you have people like this in your life, that's great.

Now, imagine me as a conservative that is against gay people. What if I said that being gay was against my religion and that I didn't accept gay people? What if I said "I'm not homophobic but gay people are sick people. They should be cured of their gay disease."

To be honest, it's sounds hypocritical because you're saying that you're not homophobic, but you're saying something that is homophobic. The same thing applies to transphobic comments. Below, I will list some comments that I hear from people. Sometimes, people say them without meaning to be rude. However, there are people who will say them on purpose. Here is my list of comments, positive and negative.

1. No matter what, I'll support you 100%.

2. Congratulations for coming out.

3. You were born a man/woman, so you should stay a man/woman.

4. I'm against sex change because that's tampering with God's creation.

5. You will never be a real man/woman. If you have a penis, you're a man. If you don't have a penis, you're a woman.

6. That was very brave if you to come out. How do your friends and family handle it?

First of all, tampering with God's creation is what humans do. We domesticated animals and plants for our desired traits and weeded out the ones that we didn't like. We also genetically engineered organisms to be more useful to humans. They are not natural species because they have been created by humans. So technically, we can't say that we are against being unnatural. Being unnatural is not always a bad thing. I think that it has benefited humans and has helped us live the life we live today. Although, there are pros and cons to everything.

I can't argue with the fact that I will never be a biological male, just like a transgender woman will never be a biological female. In order to align our bodies with our gender identity, we inject hormones and get surgeries to help us pass as our identified gender. In cases, including my own, it has helped reduced gender disforia and has helped me feel more comfortable in my body. Since I can't produce testosterone at a level of a biological male, I have to inject synthetic testosterone every three weeks. Hormone doses may vary for different people and their bodies may react differently.

If you are a transgender person who wants to start hormones, do your research first. Get a referral to an endocrinologist if you are 100% sure that this is what you want to do. Please think before you decide because the hormones will have side affects. Your bodies may react differently

to the hormones than other bodies, including my own.

Pros and cons of being a Transgender Man

Here are the pros to being a transgender man. First of all, I never have to worry about wet dreams. I also never have to worry about accidentally getting a woman pregnant if I end up having sex with her. I understand why ladies do not like men leaving their toilet seat lifted up. Since I've gone through female puberty, I can relate better to women.

However, the cons are knowing that I will never be able to produce sperm. This means that I will never be able to be a biological father. I will never have the same anatomy that a biological male person has. I can still get periods if I still have my female reproductive organs. Whenever I use the bathroom, I have to be extra cautious because there may be transphobic people who are against transgender men using the men's room.

I'm glad I never have to worry about wet dreams. After all, I can't produce seamen. I never have to wake up with my bed wet. I can't imagine how embarrassing it would be, especially for a teenage boy.

I'm glad I never have to worry about accidentally impregnating a woman. If she tries to tell people that I fathered her baby, I would make sure to back up my claim with evidence about why it's impossible for me to be a biological father. I would also back up my claim with proofs. Then, she can't lie about me fathering her child. She cannot try to trap me into paying child support for the next eighteen years.

However, realizing that I can't produce sperm is depressing at times because I'll never be able to biologically father children. However, that's the fact and I have to accept it. Well, there's other options if my future partner and I wanted to have children. We could adopted or use a sperm donor. I am planning for her to carry the pregnancy to term. I don't think I can handle labour and delivery because it sounds scary. I've never been interested in carrying the baby. After reading my biology textbook, I never ever wanted to experience labour. I read about how the procedure is done. I had a nightmare about it once. I was in one of the bathrooms at my parents' house and I ended up giving birth to a dead baby. I will make sure that I don't have to go through childbirth.

I think that being pregnant would trigger disforia. After all, I always think to myself, "Men don't get pregnant and bear children."

As a transgender man, having my period is terrible. I always get depressed when it happens. I always think to myself, "Men don't get periods." Every month, I always wonder when it's going to stop. I always have to have supplies just in case it happens.

I thing that cisgender men take it for granted because they easily pass as men. Transgender men, like myself have to work harder in order to pass. We have to get referred for hormones, change our name and gender on our identification documents, and consider whether to have surgery. Also, when we inject testosterone, our bodies need time to get used to it. First of all, testosterone is not the main hormone that we produce. It's estrogen. The testosterone we inject is synthetic. It's not natural to our bodies.

Imagine a transgender woman taking estrogen. Her body mainly produces testosterone because she has a male body. If she went through male puberty, a lot of the physical changes would be irreversible, such as the deepening of the voice and facial hair.

Advice for Parents of Transgender Children

I think the best think you can do is to learn how to accept your child's gender identity. I know it can be hard as parents because you've raised them for years in the gender they were assigned at birth. Trust me, it wasn't easy for my parents when I first came out to them. My dad especially had a hard time dealing with the change. He refused to use male pronouns and he still called me by my birth name.

My mom had an easier time because she was more open minded than my dad was. She would slip up and use female pronouns and my birth name. I always corrected her every time. The way she explained this was that she was so used to calling me by my birth name for over twenty years and it was hard for her to adapt. I had no patience when I first came out. I just accepted my family to get used to it right away, including my own parents.

Coming out to my family has taught me how to be patient with them. Also, it taught me how to live as my true self and empowered me to help other people accept themselves. I also learned how to increase my self esteem and have more self confidence.

My name change has been hard for my parents. I find that a lot of parents have a hard time when their child decides to change their name. First of all, it is understandable for parents to struggle with this. I'm not a parent myself, but I've watched my parents go through the transition of my name change. I wanted my parents to understand that changing my name would align my identity with my gender.

If your child chooses to change their legal name, it's very important to learn how to accept that this is what they want to do. Support them, even though you don't agree with their name change. No matter what, they want your support and acceptance. If you had a transgender child who has or is going to change their name, you probably feel betrayed. After all, you've chosen their name for them when they were babies.

Of course we don't choose our own names when we are babies. However, as we get older, we can either choose to keep our name or change it. It's up to us when we are adults. Name change is especially important to transgender people because it helps us feel more aligned with our psychological gender. For example: I chose the name Thomas because that name defines who I am. It is a very masculine name and I do identify as masculine.

Before your child goes through the name change process, start referring to them by their new name. Also, encourage other family members and friends to start calling your child by that name. When the name is officially changed, they will be used to it by then.

If your child is under the age of majority, you will need to provide consent in order to have your child's name change. When they are over the age of majority, they can do it without a parent. If you want to find out more about how the name change process works, go to your registry.

Remember that this is a big change for you too. You're getting used to your child changing their identity. It's not going to be easy at first. There will be ups and downs. You will feel confused and overwhelmed at first. Eventually, you'll learn how to get used to the change. It's not going to happen overnight. Everything takes time.

It'll be strange for you to call your kid by their new name. It won't feel the same. You'll feel hurt and sad. You may feel angry. When your child is an adult, the best thing to do is to go along with their decision to come out to you. Listen to your child. It's probably hard as parents to listen to their children. It's also difficult for children to listen to their parents. I stress the

importance of both children and parents listening to each other. It gives both sides the chance to

put themselves in each other's shoes. h

Is My Child Too Young to Transition?

It really depends. Some transition earlier than others. The best answer is when your child is ready to transition. When they transition at a really young age, there is no need to worry about surgery and hormones yet. You can help them transition socially and allow them to live in the opposite gender than the one assigned at birth.

Talk to other parents so you can build a support network. It may help you deal with the challenges of having a transgender child. It'll give you a chance to make new friends. Make sure to find people who are positive. Do not make friends with parents who will criticize you because of the fact you have a transgender child.

Jazz Jennings is a transgender girl who transitioned at the age of five with the support of her parents. At that age, she knew that she was a girl born in the wrong body. You can learn more about her on the show, "I am Jazz." In this show, you get to see what her life is like and how she deals with negative attitudes toward her. Her parents and siblings support her.

I think everyone discovers their gender identity at different ages. I didn't discover my gender identity until I was twelve. It only grew stronger and persisted as I got older.

Going through female puberty was terrible. the worst thing about it was having to deal with periods. I got emotional easily. I think that it was because of the estrogen going through my brain. I honestly regret going through female puberty, but there's nothing I can do now. If I knew about hormone blockers at an earlier age, I would have convinced my parents to let me take them. I would not have to go through female puberty. When I was nine, I noticed that I was developing breast buds. I had no idea what was going on. I had to wear a training bra at eleven. That was when my mom told me that growing breasts was part of becoming a woman.

When your transgender child approaches the age of puberty, talk to them about hormone blockers. What hormone blockers do is put puberty on pause until your child decide to go on hormones. Hormone blockers are reversible, but hormones are not. Hormone blockers can be given as a shot or as a pump inserted into your arm. Speak to your child's doctor if you and your child is considering hormone blockers. I would not suggest having your child start hormones while they are still growing. Hormones can stunt their growth. For example: when your transgender daughter takes estrogen, her growth plates will close after she begins taking it.

If your child wants to begin hormones, have their doctor refer them to an endocrinologist. Discourage them from purchasing hormones from unreliable sources. In order for your child to begin hormones, the endocrinologist has to prescribe them. Also, your child's blood work needs to be done. Also note that hormones have side affects. The endocrinologist will inform you about them. Note that it is not my job to tell you what the side effects are. I'm not a doctor.

Once your child gets approved for hormones, the endocrinologist will normally start on a low dose. Their body needs to get used to the hormones because they are not natural to the body. If you have a transgender son, his body will mainly produce estrogen if he still has his female reproductive organs. With a transgender daughter, her body would mainly produce testosterone if she still has her male reproductive organs. So she has to get used to the estrogen put in her body. On the other hand, a transgender man has to get testosterone injected into his body.

As a transgender man myself, I can tell you that it is possible for me to have periods and get pregnant while I'm on testosterone. Every transgender man's body is different, so their bodies may react to hormones differently. The side affects I face are mood swings, aggressiveness, and anger. After I increased my dose from 70 mG to 100 mG per three weeks, my mood swings were all over the place. Your transgender son may face some or all of the side affects of taking testosterone.

The most common for of testosterone administration is by a needle. He may get it injected on his butt or thigh. Note that more testosterone does not mean that he'll develop male characteristics faster. He should take the dose that the doctor puts him on. Too high of a dose will cause issues. A dose that is too high will be too much for his body to metabolize. Testosterone gets converted into estrogen.

A Note To Minors

If you seriously want to transition to the opposite sex or gender, it's really important to think about it. Don't rush into making major decisions, such as hormones and surgery. Please do your research before deciding to change your body. There's plenty of time to explore your identity. You may be a tomboy, a girl that likes to do typically masculine stuff. You may be a feminine boy. If you are 100% sure that you identify as the opposite gender, then go ahead and make a plan to come out to your family and friends.

It takes a lot of emotional and psychological maturity to have the capacity to make life altering decisions, such as choosing to have surgery, changing your identity, and socially transitioning. To be honest, I'm bias about little kids wanting to transition. First of all, they are not mature enough to understand what being transgender is. They don't have the mental capacity to make major decisions. I disagree with the book called "I am Jazz" because a lot of things Jazz Jennings says in her book are inaccurate. As a baby, you don't know your gender identity yet. You just came out of your mom and you haven't experienced the world outside her uterus. I disagree with the term, "Assigned Sex", unless I'm referring to intersex people. This is because our sex chromosomes determine our biological sex. XY chromosomes produce a male offspring and XX chromosomes produce female offspring. This usually determines our phenotypical sex. Usually, our psychological sex matches our biological sex. In transgender people, they are biologically one sex but they are psychologically the opposite sex.

If you're in your teen years and you are 100% sure that you want to transition, please keep in mind the pros and cons. Every decision we make has consequences, positive and negative. When choosing to start hormones, ask yourself the following questions:

Am I for sure ready to come out to my parents, friends, and teachers?

How will transitioning benefit me?

How will taking hormones affect my body and mind?

Do I want to have kids?

Am I ready to start surgery?

How will being transgender affect my sex life?

Will I be surrounded by people who are supportive and accepting?

There are great resources on the internet about being transgender. However, there are also unreliable sources, such as Wikipedia. Go on YouTube and hear from Transgender individuals, such as Ty Turner. They will be able to give you their perspectives on being transgender. Look for credible websites and peer reviewed articles when searching on the internet.

Also, consider how coming out will affect you at your part time job and school. Be sure you're in a safe place before you come out. If you're not in a safe place, you will likely face bullying. You will run the risk of being rejected my your friends and family. Unfortunately, there are kids who get kicked out for coming out.

It's important to be aware of statistics of transgender people. Make sure you don't end up in the position of committing suicide. It's not worth it. You're not doing anyone a favour. Instead, you are causing people to suffer from your loss. Unfortunately, transgender people are more likely to kill themselves. This statistic is disturbing.

I cannot stress enough about the importance of mental health. I find that mental health is often ignored in the Asian culture. I find that people in this culture do not believe in mental health disorders. I think it's hard for a lot of us to understand the concept of psychology.

If you're having mental health issues, talk to a school councillor. It's important to have someone who will be able to help you manage stress, anxiety, and depression effectively. Your doctor may prescribe medication to help you deal with your mental health issues.

How the Gender Change Process Works

Are you a transgender person who is in the process of getting your gender change on your ID documents? If you are considering this, it's a complicated and long process. Policies may vary. Generally, you need a letter from a doctor from The College of Physicians or a psychologist from the College of Psychologists. confirming your request for the gender change. In some places, you may also need a confirmation of the gender reassignment surgery. Honestly, I think that this sounds outdated because our gender is not the same as our biological sex. After you submit your doctor's letter to the registry, you need to fill out an affidavit swearing that this is what you are doing. It's important to be patient because this is a very long process. It'll get done. Once it's over, it'll be official.

It may take up to two weeks to get your new driver's license or ID card in the mail. Your birth certificate may take up to two months. If you live in Alberta, you don't need confirmation of the sex change to change your gender on your documents. If you are under the age of majority, you need your parents or legal guardians to help you with this process. The challenging part is that they can refuse to have your gender changed on your legal documents. If they refuse, wait until you reach the age of majority. If they disapprove, they will not have control over the decision; you have the control. Once you reach the age of majority, the law defines you as an adult. However, being an adult is not about turning 18 years old and having the freedom to do whatever you want. You have to consider consequences when making decisions. You have to be responsible with your decisions and learn how to make adult decisions. Also, you are expected to behave like an adult, especially when you enter the adult world.

If the gender change is what you want to do for sure, then get started on it. Transition will go easier if you have people you support such as your family, friends, councillors, professors, etc. It's important to have people that will be accepting of your transgender identity.

When I was getting my gender change on my ID, it took me three times to get the doctor to include necessary information in order for the registry to complete the process. I only waited about two weeks for the new ID with my new gender on it. The challenging part was going through the process of changing my gender on my birth certificate. I had to wait for the affidavit to come in the mail. After it came in the mail, I had to bring it to the registry with another copy of my doctor's letter. I had to sign the affidavit and swear to God that I wanted to change my gender to male and I would maintain that gender.

If you got your gender changed legally, I want to congratulate you for being patient to go through the process. If you change your gender to align your gender with what you identify, you will less likely be misread as the other gender. This is because your ID will display your new gender instead of the one assigned at birth. Personally, I hated showing my ID because it still read "female." I had issues with that during my early months of transition. Now, my ID and birth certificate had my gender marker changed. Next, I had the gender marker changed on my Alberta Health card. This made things easier because now, my gender marker on my ID documents matched my gender identity.

I suggest doing the name change first before you change your gender on your legal documents. This is my preference. However, if you have everything for changing them both at the same time, then go ahead and do it. I personally got my name changed first so that people could have time to get used to the new name It's a relief that my ID says "male" and I don't have to worry about people misgendering me when they read it. Now, I am legally male on my ID. Once I get my gender on my health care card changed, things will go a lot more smoothly for me. People would not be as confused because all of my documents will say "male."

Dating Challenges as a Transgender Man

I have trouble with dating as a transgender man because I always have anxiety issues about it. I often fear that some women wouldn't be okay with dating a transgender guy because he has a female body. If a woman accepts me for who I am, then I want to marry her. call me old school, but I'm not interested in dating. I'm more interested in a long term relationship, which is marriage. If women are not accepting of me, I just know they are not right for me.

I often fear that women wouldn't be into me because of my height. I find that women prefer men who are at least six feet tall. I'm stuck at five feet tall, or 152 cm. Sometimes, I wish I was five feet and ten inches like Rod Rash, my old math teacher. That's the height I would want to be at. Well, I just have to accept that I will never be a tall man.

Honestly, I'm in no rush when it comes to finding women to marry. I just have to make sure that I find the one that I will be with for the rest of my life. I honestly do not need to rush. I honestly do not care about her race. What matters to me is that she is healthy and in good shape. I also want a woman who takes care of her hygiene.

I don't like party girls because they are too much trouble. They are the kind of women I would not marry. I don't want a girl who doesn't take her life seriously or drinks to much. I also don't want a girl who needs to go clubbing every night, every weekend, and so on.

If I am in a relationship, I want to make sure that the woman that I am with is okay with a transgender man. I will disclose myself to her so that she knows that I am transgender. If I don't find a woman until I'm in my thirties, I'm okay with that. The day will come. I'm still looking for women.

What I want to tell people is that being transgender doesn't make me a freak. I want to be treated just like how other guys are treated. What I don't want is to be treated like a woman just because I have female parts. I'm pretty sure that transgender women want to be treated like other women. It's the same idea. I want people to respect my gender identity. I want to be referred by male pronouns. If you are not familiar with the term, "transgender", it's important to educate yourselves about what it means. I find it disrespectful when people, especially my parents, purposely refer to me by my birth name. I'm sorry, but this is not the name I identify with anymore. I remember when my dad was still referring to me by my birth name. I often confronted him and asked him not to refer me by that name.

If you have relatives or friends who are gender nonconforming, it's really important to respect them for who they are. They are still human beings, just like the rest of us are. Respect their preferences on what they want to be referred to. That will show them that you have respect for them and that you are willing to be supportive. I understand that this may take some time. The reality is that everything takes time to get used to.

When is a good time to Transition?

It depends. The best time is whenever you are ready to. Make sure that you are in a safe

place and time before you start to transition. I know it can be scary at first. Before you start to

transition, do some research. What I mean is lots and lots of research. Don't be in such a rush.

Make sure you have all the information needed before you start to come out to your family and

friends as transgender. If you are in grade school or university, make sure to let your teachers or

professors know. Personally, my professors have been very accepting, especially Rod Rash,

Michael Buhr, and John O'Connor. Without them, I wouldn't have the courage to continue to live

my life so that I could be what I want to be. They've had my back when I was in a really dark

place. They were concerned for me when I told them about suicide thoughts. They reached out to

the Student Life office. I really appreciated that they were caring.

Being transgender has made me who I am. I don't consider this as a disorder. Rather, I

think of being transgender as being unique. Being transgender has taught me that gender is in the

brain, not in our biology. I also learned that gender does not have to match sex.

If you are considering surgery, make sure to really think things through. Surgery is

irreversible and it can make you sterile. Also, think about whether you want to have children in

the future. For transgender women, I advise you to store your sperm if you want to have children.

For transgender men, think about whether you want to keep your female reproductive organs or

not. This is a big decision and we have to decide carefully.

The best time to have surgery is whenever you're ready. If you really want to start

surgery, make sure to see a psychiatrist first. Surgery is a long and complicated process. There are different types of surgery such as chest reconstruction surgery. There are also different ways surgeons can construct a vagina for transgender women and a penis for transgender men. It's best to ask the surgeon what kinds of SRS are available. I will not go into detail about the medical terms because I am not a doctor. However, you need to consider the pros and cons. Keep in mind that there are risks, including complications. Expect that it may take a long time for you to recover.

If you are a transgender woman who is considering taking estrogen, make sure to get a hold of an endocrinologist first. Also, consider the benefits and risks of taking estrogen. When you take estrogen, you will start to grow breasts and your body fat will distribute into more of a female pattern. Your sperm count may decrease. Your muscle mass may decrease. However, estrogen will not make your voice go higher. It will also not make your facial hair go away. I am sorry to say this, but you will not get periods.

If you want to pass as female, it can be challenging because your voice sounds like a man's voice. You can get training so you can learn how to make your voice sound more feminine. I don't know too much about it myself. I recommend for you to check out Julie Vou's YouTube channel. She is a transgender woman. She is also Vietnamese. She began transitioning in her teen years. She had to get voice training to learn how to talk like a woman. She explains about her bottom surgery. She talks about why it is important to dilate to keep her vagina open.

As a transgender man who wants to start testosterone, your voice will start to deepen. Also, your sex drive will increase and your body odour will smell. However, testosterone has the risk of raising the level of bad cholesterol and you could become sterile. However, it is still possible to get periods while you are on testosterone. Pregnancy can also be possible. Also, testosterone increases blood cell count.

Note that taking more testosterone does not mean that your changes will happen at a faster rate. Your body actually converts the excess testosterone into estrogen. This is why it's important to be patient. I recommend that you get your testosterone by injection because it is the least expensive and the most effective method. I get my testosterone by injection every three weeks and I notice some changes to my body. It is like being a teen again because I am going through a second puberty. I noticed my appetite increase and my voice starting to deepen. I also started growing facial hair.

Some people also take testosterone by patch. What it does is slowly release the hormones through your skin.. However, it's not the most effective at stopping periods. One thing that you should not do is take testosterone orally because it is toxic to the liver. It is not recommended.

While you are on testosterone, make sure that you give your body time to adjust. Remember, your body mainly produces estrogen. So, if you introduce testosterone to your body, the testosterone will compete with the female hormones already present. Overtime, your estrogen levels will be reduced to a male level. It may take time for your periods to stop. All you can do is hope that you will not have them, unless you have your female reproductive organs removed. Also, make sure to get your blood work done.

If you happened to be pregnant, stop taking testosterone. Testosterone is toxic to the baby. Make sure that you find doctors who are transgender friendly and who are okay with helping a transgender man give birth. If you are planning to take testosterone again, wait until you're not pregnant and refer to your endocrinologist.

Note that testosterone is not a form of birth control. If you're having sex with a biologically male person, including a transgender woman, you may still get pregnant. There are non-hormonal birth control options available. Please use condoms. They protect against STI's and unwanted pregnancies.

The most important advice to give is never let anyone discourage you from living as your true self. You should not feel ashamed for being who you are. This applies to anyone, not just transgender people. If you have a group of supportive people you know, you will have a much easier time coming out to them. If you don't have a support group, coming out will be harder. If you don't have a supportive group of friends and family, tell a school councillor or a psychologist. If you have any thoughts of suicide, tell a councillor or call a distress line. Don't try to kill yourself. Remember, we only have one chance to live and we need to enjoy what life has to offer.

Remember, you are what you are. We do not choose our gender identity. I believe that it is wired into our brain. I also believe that gender is in the mind rather than in the biology. Most of us know our gender from the time we are little, while others don't discover it until later in their life.

Unfortunately, a lot of transgender people are not accepted by their family. Often, parents come from an old mentality. of thinking. Their views tend to be conservative. Christians often are transphobic. They are taught to believe what the bible says. They believe that God wants us to live with the sex we are designed at birth. They also say that God does not want us to switch gender.

I respect some aspects of religion. However, I find that people who are religious do not tolerate people who are lesbian, gay, bisexual, trans, and queer. Unfortunately, parents kick their kids out for coming out as gay. Some parents go as far as disowning them. After all, didn't God say for us to respect one another? Didn't God also say to love each other? As human beings, we tend to judge one another. I'm no exception.

When transgender people are not accepted, they are at a higher chance of committing suicide. So are people who are gay and lesbian. Jazz mentioned that about 40% of transgender people commit suicide because they are often alienated by people they know.

What I suggest that people do is keep their opinions to themselves if they discriminate others. We are entitled to our opinions and beliefs. However, if they hurt others, then they shouldn't be said. Also, we cannot change the way other people think. The only person we can control is ourselves. I've read "The 7 Habits of Highly Effective Teens," by Sean Covey. It was recommended to me by my high school EA. As a teenager, this concept was the hardest to grasp. I would often try to change the way my peers thought. The same thing applies to people who are not accepting of the LGTBQ people.

If people around you are transphobic, it's important that you give them time to process that fact that you came out to them. If your family finally accepts you, great. If not, You're stuck with them until you move out. You're going to have to deal with it, even though you wanted them to accept you. If you ever get kicked out of your home because of rejection from your family, you need to find a place to stay at temporarily until you find your own apartment. Stay in your car if you can. Also, find a shelter. If you're working and you have enough money for a hotel, stay at a hotel. But don't stay their permanently because hotels charge every night. They are expensive. If a hotel charges you $100 per night and you stay there for 30 days straight, the hotel would cost you $3000 for 30 days. That is a lot of money.

If your friends ever reject you because you are transgender, it's time to find new friends. Meet people at your school, work place, social event, etc. It's really important to have good friends. As humans, we are social creatures.

If your college or university has an option for you to have your preferred name on your student ID, you should talk to them about how the process works. If you are in the process of getting your name legally changed, take advantage of this option. If your school insists that your birth name be on the ID card, wait until your legal name change is processed. Once the process is complete, take your name change certificate and birth certificate and show it to the registrar. They need to see proof that your name has been legally changed. Also, get the name on your government issued ID or driver's licence changed. To change the name on your passport, you need to apply for a new one.

Let your professors know of any name change if they knew you by your previous name. If you have new professors, they won't know about your birth name. They'll just know you by your current name. That way, it's a brand new start.

If your boss and co-workers know you by your previous name, please let them know of the changes. First, notify your boss as soon as you know that the change was processed. They also may want to see a proof of name change. That way, all of your pay cheques and pay stubs will be written in your current name.

Check out other websites that explain about what transgender is. Here are some links that you can check out. Also, if you go on YouTube, check out transgender people such as Jazz Jennings, Ty Turner, and others. Jazz Jennings is a transgender girl who transitioned at the age of five. She has a show called "I am Jazz". Ty turner is a transgender man who started hormones and transitioning at age seventeen. You can also learn about Thomas Beatie, the transgender man who decided to get pregnant. He is known as the pregnant man. He began transitioning at age twenty-four and started hormones in the early 2000's.

If you want to learn more about any of the transgender people I mentioned, look them up on YouTube. There are lots of videos about them. Ty turner has his own YouTube channel and he posts very informative videos. Thomas Beatie has videos on his YouTube channel about his pregnancy journey and raising children with his wife, Nancy. Also, check out Jazz Jennings on YouTube. She has some great videos on her YouTube channel.

Below, I try to provide reliable resources to help educate you about being transgender. Please do not use this information as medical advice from the doctor. This is just for educational purposes only.

FTM Guide - How to change your gender from female to male!

ftm-guide.com/

Everything You Wanted to Know About Being a Trans Man but Were ...

https://www.huffingtonpost.com/.../everything-you-wanted-to-know-about-being-a-tr...

Hormones - Transgender Health Information Program

transhealth.phsa.ca › Medical

Hormone therapy for transgender patients - NCBI - NIH

https://www.ncbi.nlm.nih.gov/pmc/articles/PMC5182227/

Information on Estrogen Hormone Therapy | Transgender Care

https://transcare.ucsf.edu/article/information-estrogen-hormone-therapy

Transgender Health & Transitioning | Revel & Riot

www.revelandriot.com/resources/trans-health/

Metabolic Effects of Hormone Therapy in Transgender Patients

https://www.ncbi.nlm.nih.gov/pmc/articles/PMC4824309/

For FTM Singers:

Transgender Men, Testosterone, and Singing: Some Advice

https://www.eliconley.com › blog › transgender-men-testo...
https://www.eliconley.com › blog › transgender-men-testo...

The Singing Voice During the First Two Years of Testosterone ...

https://scholar.colorado.edu › downloads
https://scholar.colorado.edu

Acknowledgements

I thank my mom and sisters for being supportive throughout my transition. This is why I am the confident person I am today. I understand that it was hard for them, but they did a good job of handling the transition. If I didn't have support, I wouldn't be where I am now.

I also thank some of my professors, John O'Connor, Glenn Binington, Rod Rash, and Michael Buhr. When I was in a dark place, they reached out to ensure that I wasn't going to do anything that would put my life at risk. I am very fortunate to have professors who care.

It wasn't easy coming out as my true self at first. However, gaining knowledge about transgender identity gave me the power to educate people about what it's like to have the body of one gender and the mind of another. I often researched on the internet and read about this on several websites such as Huffington Post, Female to Male, etc. I also got this information from reading the Readers Digest magazine. Without doing research, I wouldn't have the courage to come out and transition from female to male.

I wrote this book to help the general public understand what being transgender is. I also did this to help other transgender individuals find the courage to come out and learn how to build a network of supportive people. The people in the network can be family members, friends, professors, teachers, co-workers, etc. The point of this book is to teach people to think of gender, rather as a spectrum instead of as a binary category. I also want to say that being transgender is nothing to be ashamed of. This is just how God made us.

I want to thank you for taking time to read this book. I hope you learned from it. I would recommend this book to your transgender friends or family members.

Dedicated to:

- John O'Connor

- Michael Buhr

- Glenn Binnington

- Rod Rash

- Angela Roppo

Made in the USA
Middletown, DE
11 January 2022